Who Was Aretha Franklin?

by Nico Medina

illustrated by Gregory Copeland

Penguin Workshop

For my editor, Paula K. Manzanero, with much respect—NM

To Deb, Mary, and Lisa, for all you do—GC

PENGUIN WORKSHOP
An Imprint of Penguin Random House LLC, New York

Published by Penguin Workshop, an imprint of Penguin Random House LLC, New York.
PENGUIN and PENGUIN WORKSHOP are trademarks of Penguin Books Ltd.
WHO HQ & Design is a registered trademark of Penguin Random House LLC.
Printed in the USA.

Visit us online at www.penguinrandomhouse.com.

Library of Congress Cataloging-in-Publication Data is available upon request.

ISBN 9780451532398 (paperback) 10 9 8
ISBN 9780451532411 (library binding) 10 9 8 7 6 5 4 3 2

Contents

Who Was Aretha Franklin?

New Bethel Baptist Church on Hastings Street in Detroit, Michigan, was more than a church to its all-black congregation. To those who worshipped there, it was the center of their community—a safe space to praise the Lord with their friends and neighbors.

Outside the church walls, the world could be cruel, a place where black people were often treated unfairly. But every Sunday, they gathered at New Bethel to hear the inspiring words of their passionate minister, Reverend C. L. Franklin.

They also came for the music.

One Sunday in 1952, Reverend Franklin's ten-year-old daughter, Aretha, sang her first solo. As a member of New Bethel Baptist Church's junior choir, Aretha had sung at

Sunday services before—but only with the choir. Never alone.

The large church held 2,500 people. Not everyone could see Aretha, so she stood on a chair. When she opened her mouth to sing . . . *everyone* could hear her!

Aretha sang her solo in "Sealed to the Day of Redemption." The song is about a person whose "life was a wreck" until the day of redemption,

the day when some Christians hope to meet Jesus in Heaven.

Aretha's voice soared. The congregation was moved. They felt the spirit of the Lord in her voice. "Amen!" they called. They clapped their hands. They stomped their feet. They whooped and hollered.

This is what gospel music, the music of the black church, is all about.

Aretha had been hearing, singing, and living gospel music her whole life.

The congregation's love fed Aretha's troubled soul. She had already been through terrible heartache in her young life. Months earlier, Aretha's mother had died of a heart attack. Perhaps Aretha thought of this as she sang:

Soon Jesus will come.
And he'll take me away . . .
I'm gonna live with the saints,
in glory someday.

Aretha went on to experience more loss in her life. But she always had the special talent to channel her emotions into her soulful music. She became one of the most famous, beloved, and gifted singers in history, singing for presidents and royalty. Her songs bridged the divide between black and white popular music.

Aretha, as the future Queen of Soul, inspired a generation to demand the rights and "R-E-S-P-E-C-T" they deserved.

CHAPTER 1
Daddy the "Jazz Preacher"

Aretha Louise Franklin was born on March 25, 1942, in Memphis, Tennessee. Her family called her "Ree" for short. She had three older siblings—a sister named Erma, a brother, Cecil, and a half brother, Vaughan. Aretha's little sister, Carolyn, was born in 1944.

Clarence LaVaughan—or "C.L."—Franklin was Aretha's father. Reverend Franklin was a popular preacher known for his passionate sermons—the part of a church service that is most like a speech.

Reverend Franklin was known as the "Man with the Million-Dollar Voice." His powerful sermons incorporated speaking, shouting, and—most important—*singing*! The Franklin children looked up to their daddy. He would always be a big influence in their lives.

C. L. Franklin

Born in 1915 in Mississippi, C.L. had the voice of a grown man by the time he was ten. C.L.'s mother, Rachel (who was called Big Mama), thought the world of him. C.L. read a lot when he was a young boy, and by the time he was eighteen, he was visiting other churches around the country, preaching as far away as Cleveland, Ohio.

At twenty-one, he married Barbara Siggers, Aretha's mother. Barbara was a gifted pianist and gospel singer. Like C.L., she had grown up in Mississippi.

C. L. Franklin was among the first black preachers to use radio to reach his listeners. He hosted a radio show in Memphis called *The Shadow of the Cross*. The program gave messages of unity and inspiration to black people in the South. When the Franklins moved to Buffalo, New York, in 1944, C.L. hosted another show called *Voice of Friendship*. It featured gospel music and C.L.'s sermons. Reverend Franklin quickly became a well-known and trusted voice in black America.

In 1946, C.L. became minister at Detroit's New Bethel Baptist Church. Aretha was four years old when her family moved to Michigan. Like C.L. and Barbara, many New Bethel churchgoers also came from poor black families in the South who had moved north looking for a better life. They admired Reverend Franklin for having found success in Detroit, far from the farms of his childhood.

People came to Detroit looking for jobs, but they also came for the music.

New Bethel Baptist Church was on Hastings Street in the Black Bottom neighborhood of Detroit, the center of the city's black culture. All along the boulevard, churches stood alongside music clubs. Joe's Record Shop sold the latest jazz and blues albums, as well as recordings of C.L.'s sermons.

The Great Migration

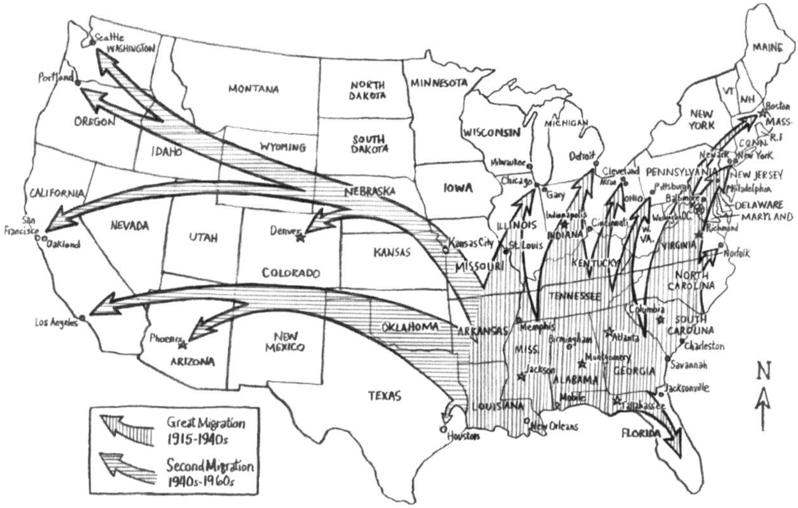

Between the years 1916 and 1970, more than six million African Americans moved from the American South to the industrial cities of the North, Midwest, and West.

When the United States entered World War I in 1917, there were factory jobs available in many Northern cities, while the South remained mostly rural farmland. And as agricultural technology improved, machines took over many of the Southern farm jobs previously done by people.

Life in the South was difficult. Segregation, the physical separation of black people and white people, was still legal there. So black Southerners left on buses, trains, boats, even horse-drawn carts. They established centers of black culture in famous neighborhoods, like Harlem in New York City and Black Bottom in Detroit. In 1900, 90 percent of African Americans lived in the South; by 1970, less than half lived there.

People who sang in the jazz and blues clubs on Friday and Saturday nights might also sing religious gospel music in church on Sunday mornings. The different types of music influenced one another. And not every preacher thought that was a good idea.

But C.L. believed that *all* good music came from God. He went to the clubs on Hastings Street and made friends with the musicians. On Sundays, they'd come to hear him preach at New Bethel. He became known as the "Jazz Preacher."

Blues, Jazz, and R&B

Blues music has its roots in the work songs of black slaves. It expressed their everyday joys and sorrows, and used some of the same rhythms as gospel music. As black people left the South, blues music took root in cities like Memphis, Chicago, and Detroit. Jazz music developed as a mixture of black and white folk music at about the same time as the blues. It featured an irregular beat, with improvised, unplanned melodies. Blues and jazz mixed together and helped give rise to R&B, or "rhythm and blues," in the 1940s.

Jazz

The Franklin children grew up in the church, learning from their father's sermons and singing hymns along with the church choir. Aretha was a shy girl, and she looked up to the gospel singers. Maybe she'd grow up to be just like them.

One day at a funeral service, one of C.L.'s good friends, Clara Ward, was singing the hymn "Peace in the Valley." Clara Ward was one of the most respected gospel singers in the country. During the song, Clara became so overcome with passion that she took off her church hat and threw it to the ground! She was communicating the emotion of the song with her voice and her whole body.

When Aretha saw how strongly the music affected Clara Ward, she knew she wanted to be a singer, too.

CHAPTER 2
Big Changes

When Aretha was six, her mother, Barbara, moved back to Buffalo, New York, with her brother Vaughan. Ree was heartbroken. She was a very quiet girl, and she and her mother had been very close. Now they were hundreds of miles apart.

Aretha, Cecil, Erma, and Carolyn would travel to Buffalo to visit their mom. Ree so looked forward to these trips that she would pack up her suitcase days before they left. She looked forward to singing with her mother at the piano.

Aretha loved these trips to Buffalo. And as much as she loved and admired her daddy, coming back home to Detroit was hard.

The Franklin family lived at 649 East Boston Boulevard, in an elegant six-bedroom mansion in the North End neighborhood of Detroit. The area was integrated, which meant both black and white families lived there.

Reverend Franklin was a very busy man, so he hired housekeepers to help Aretha's grandmother, who lived with them, too. Big Mama was a no-nonsense woman who loved her grandchildren deeply and did her best to keep them in line.

The Franklin children and Big Mama were used to Reverend Franklin's famous friends visiting the big house on East Boston Boulevard. When Mahalia Jackson, the most famous gospel singer in the world, would stop by, she'd often walk right into the kitchen and start cooking for the family! She felt right at home boiling up a pot of collard greens.

Mahalia Jackson (1911–1972)

Mahalia Jackson was born in New Orleans and was singing in church by the time she was four. She once said, "I sing God's music because it makes me feel free. It gives me hope. With the blues, when you finish, you still have the blues."

Mahalia Jackson moved to Chicago and went on to record many albums for Columbia Records. She was the first gospel singer to perform in New York's Carnegie Hall. She became known as the Queen of Gospel, and her song "Move On Up a Little Higher" became the highest-selling gospel single in history.

Even though Aretha missed her mother dearly, she sometimes felt like a princess living in a fairy tale in that big, yellow-brick house. She loved the mansion's emerald-green carpeting and purple curtains. Perhaps what Aretha loved even more was the grand piano by the window.

From a young age, Aretha showed a natural talent for music. She listened to jazz records with her brother, Cecil, for hours. After hearing a song once, she could play it on the piano, note for note, and sing along, word for word. Music brought Aretha out of her shyness.

Sometimes she'd play songs from the radio, and her sisters and brother would join in and sing and laugh late into the evening. Later in life, Aretha would say she never wanted those nights to end.

Reverend Franklin hired a piano teacher for Aretha, but she hated the strict lessons. When she would see the piano teacher's car pulling into the driveway, she'd run and hide! She wanted to play piano her own way.

C. L. Franklin knew all the most famous singers and musicians in Detroit. Some nights, after the clubs on Hastings Street closed, he threw late-night parties that filled the house with music. Aretha and Cecil would sneak out of bed and sit at the top of the staircase to listen to these intimate jam sessions. Famous people like Duke Ellington, Ella Fitzgerald, and blues legend B. B. King were sometimes performing in their own living room!

Sometimes, as the party wound down, C.L. would go upstairs to wake Aretha. He wanted her to come downstairs and play one of his favorite blues songs, "After Hours." Reverend Franklin was proud of Aretha's talent, and his famous friends were always amazed. Everyone thought Aretha had a real gift.

When Aretha was just nine years old, she experienced a painful loss. Her daddy called the Franklin children to the kitchen to deliver the terrible news. Their mother had passed away of a heart attack. Barbara Siggers Franklin was just thirty-four.

Aretha was crushed. She could barely speak for weeks. The only thing that seemed to bring her back out of her quiet sadness was music.

Months later, when Aretha sang her first solo at church, she poured her feelings into the song. The congregation loved her for it. Their cheers and applause boosted her spirits. Aretha's voice, her natural talent, had been made even stronger by her deep feelings of love and loss.

CHAPTER 3
Aretha Hits the Road

Aretha's father fully supported her singing. He gave her Clara Ward and Mahalia Jackson records.

And whenever Ree sang a solo in church, he paid her fifteen dollars. That was a lot of money in 1952! Aretha quickly saved up and bought herself a pair of fancy roller skates. She loved going to the skating rink after school.

In the summers, Reverend Franklin took his church sermons and music on the road in a traveling gospel show. The reverend, along with a choir and famous gospel singers like Clara Ward and the Staples Singers, performed in churches and theaters, and at fairs, gospel conventions, and radio stations all across the South—and as

far away as California. Reverend Franklin reached many black Americans on these summer tours.

When Aretha was twelve, her father took her on the road with him. She was the opening act, singing with the choir or alone at the piano. Sometimes, Aretha played alongside her father during his passionate sermons. Word got around quickly of young Aretha Franklin's incredible voice. Soon, she was the main attraction at Reverend Franklin's shows. It was "great training," Aretha later said, working with these "gospel giants."

But life on the road could be difficult. The bus ride between shows might take up to ten hours!

And because of segregation, it was hard to find restaurants that would serve black people. In the 1950s, the lives of black people and white people in the United States were very separate. Hotels were segregated, too, so the gospel troupe often stayed in black boardinghouses miles off the main road.

Aretha was growing up fast, and sometimes living the life of an adult. She spent much of her time in the company of musicians and singers. Although Aretha's father believed in her singing talent and musical skills, he was often too busy running the show to mind her. Sometimes he flew between stops on the tour, leaving Aretha to ride the bus with the rest of the group.

Although it seems hard to imagine, Aretha had two children at a very young age: Clarence, who was born in 1955, and Edward, who was born two years later. Aretha's family was supportive. Her grandmother, Big Mama, believed that all babies were blessings. She raised the boys while Aretha went to school and traveled with her father during the summers.

By 1956, C. L. Franklin had sold more than half a million records of his sermons. He was famous around the country, and the Franklins were doing very well. The family moved to an even bigger and fancier house.

By now, Aretha wanted to make a record of her own. Her first recording was made during a live performance in Oakland, California. She sang two hymns: "Precious Lord, Take My Hand" and "Never Grow Old."

Back home in Detroit, Aretha recorded her first full-length album, *Songs of Faith*, live at New Bethel Baptist Church. The album of nine songs was released in 1956, when Aretha was fourteen. From the opening notes of the first track, teenage Aretha sounds every bit the mature, powerful woman.

In "Never Grow Old," Aretha sings about Heaven. Aretha's voice builds as she nears the end of the song. She draws out the words, hitting the notes high and loud. The audience cheers and shouts their approval. "Oh, yeah!" one man yells. "Never, *never*!" someone cries out as Aretha sings about the "land where we'll never grow old."

By now, Reverend Franklin had given Aretha a raise—fifty dollars for every performance. Aretha used her money to buy all kinds of records.

In 1957, fifteen-year-old Aretha and nineteen-year-old Erma heard a new song on the car radio: "You Send Me," by Sam Cooke. Both girls had a huge crush on Sam, a famous singer with a sweet voice. The sisters told their driver to get to the nearest record store, as fast as he could. Ree and Erma listened to the record so much that their father threatened to smash it with a hammer!

Sam Cooke began his career as a gospel singer, just like Aretha. "You Send Me" was known as a crossover hit—a song by a black artist that "crossed over" to appeal to white listeners, too. Aretha was excited that a gospel singer could become popular with both black and white audiences. She dreamed of having the same kind of success one day.

Detroit was bubbling with talent in the late 1950s—and not just the friends of Reverend Franklin. In Aretha's own neighborhood, some of the brightest new stars were beginning their careers.

Smokey Robinson, Cecil Franklin's best fricnd, and Diana Ross and her group, the Supremes, were getting record deals with Motown Records.

Smokey Robinson and the Miracles

Sam Cooke (1931–1964)

Sam Cooke was born in Mississippi and grew up in Chicago. His father was a church minister. When he was fifteen, he joined a gospel group called the Soul Stirrers. After six years, he left the group to perform popular (nonreligious) music.

"You Send Me" was his first big hit, knocking Elvis Presley's "Jailhouse Rock" off the top of the charts. "Twistin' the Night Away" was another huge hit.

Sam was also a successful businessman who founded his own record label, writing and producing songs for other musicians.

His ability to sing many different styles of music, from sweet and slow ballads to popular dance songs, earned him the title King of Soul.

Smokey's song "Shop Around," recorded by his group, the Miracles, was released in 1960 and went on to sell a million copies for the record label.

Motown Records was named for its hometown, the "Motor City" (or "Motor Town") of Detroit.

Motown Records

Motown signed artists that performed a mix of R&B, rock 'n' roll, and pop—crossover music that appealed to a white audience.

In early 1960, Aretha was almost eighteen. She thought the Motown family would be a good fit for her. But Reverend Franklin wanted his daughter to sign with Columbia Records, the same record label as Mahalia Jackson. However, unlike Motown, Columbia was based in New York City. It was time for Ree to leave home.

CHAPTER 4
New York, New York!

In early 1960, Aretha and her father went to New York. They met with a friend from Detroit named Major Holley. He was a jazz musician who had attended parties at the Franklin house and remembered C.L. waking Aretha up one night to come downstairs to perform. Major Holley agreed to record a demo—a sample song—of Aretha to send to Columbia Records.

Major gathered a trio of musicians to accompany Aretha on the recording. He thought that Aretha had natural talent. He couldn't believe how mature and confident this young woman sounded. By the afternoon, they had what they needed: Aretha's recording of "Today I Sing the Blues."

The tape was given to John Hammond, an important producer at Columbia. Mr. Hammond thought Aretha had the best voice he'd heard since Billie Holiday! He signed Aretha to a six-year contract right away.

Recording sessions for Aretha's first record with Columbia began in August 1960. By now, New York had become Aretha's second home. Between visits to Detroit, she lived in different hotels and boardinghouses around the city, like the YMCA and the Chelsea Hotel.

Major Holley showed her around town. He took her to jazz clubs and introduced her to other musicians. Aretha listened to all kinds of music—pop, R&B, jazz, and Broadway show tunes.

CHELSEA
222
Chelsea

Billie Holiday (1915–1959)

Billie Holiday was a famous jazz singer-songwriter who began her career singing in nightclubs in the Harlem neighborhood of New York City. She had an easy, bluesy style. Her voice didn't have a big range—she didn't sing too low or too high—but it was an interesting, attention-grabbing voice.

Holiday's songs, like "Strange Fruit" and "God Bless the Child," became American classics. Her songs would be recorded long after her death by artists like Stevie Wonder and Amy Winehouse.

Aretha soaked it all in. She recorded a wide variety of songs. She and her father both wanted Aretha's music to appeal to as many people as possible.

John Hammond had a different vision for Aretha. He wanted her to be the next big jazz and blues star. But Aretha could sing any style of music. And she wanted to "cross over," just like Sam Cooke had done. Because Aretha, C.L., and John didn't always agree on which songs to record, the album took about six months to finish.

The album, simply titled *Aretha*, was finally released in February 1961. It included a mix of pop, blues, and jazz songs—even a version of "Over the Rainbow" from the movie *The Wizard of Oz*.

A few months earlier, Aretha had given her first live New York City performance at the Village Vanguard, the famous downtown jazz club. She performed with a trio that included Major Holley playing bass.

VANGUARD

It was Aretha's first performance for a nonchurch audience. She must have been nervous. *Billboard* magazine reported that her performance was a "success when she relaxed and sang" her "blues material," and noted the "strong gospel accent" in her voice.

Critics were impressed with Aretha's first album. *Down Beat* magazine called her "the most important female vocalist to come along in some years." The songs were played on the radio. But sales were slow, and the album didn't produce any crossover hits.

This was a tough time for Aretha. She missed her sons. And she missed her father's guidance. Aretha had plenty of friends in New York. She had been dating but hadn't really fallen in love. Then along came Ted.

Ted White was another family friend from Detroit. He had known Aretha since she was a girl. Ted and Aretha shared the same birthday, though

Ted was eleven years older. He was a handsome, confident, well-dressed man who wore custom-made suits.

Aretha and Ted fell in love and were married in 1961. Reverend Franklin was not too happy about Aretha's marriage. He didn't trust Ted.

But Aretha was an adult now. Her confidence began to grow. She dressed in more modern clothes and enjoyed going to parties with her fashionable husband.

Ted White was a businessman who had successfully managed other singers' careers. Aretha knew that Ted understood pop music better than her father did. So Ted became her new manager. He quickly booked a tour for Aretha to perform with Sam Cooke.

Reverend Franklin was very busy at this time. Much of Hastings Street, including New Bethel Baptist Church, had been torn down to build a new highway. The reverend, who preached a message of self-worth and black pride, hired an all-black construction company to rebuild his church bigger and better.

C.L. was also involved in the Civil Rights Movement, organizing demonstrations and concerts for the cause of equal rights for black

Americans. Sometimes when C.L. asked Aretha to sing at his rallies, Ted got upset. He wanted Aretha to perform at clubs where she would be paid to sing.

But as much as Aretha loved her husband, she always said yes to Reverend Franklin. She loved her father, and she believed strongly in the fight for civil rights.

The Civil Rights Movement

Nearly a century after the Emancipation Proclamation ended slavery in the United States in 1863, black Americans had not achieved full equality. Beginning in the 1950s, activists began to use nonviolent protest to bring about change.

Black people in Montgomery, Alabama, refused to ride city buses for more than a year after Rosa Parks was arrested for not giving her seat to a white man. In 1960, black students in North Carolina sat at "whites only" lunch counters until they were served (or dragged out), leading to more "sit-ins" across the South. Marches were organized across the country, including the 1963 March on Washington, where more than 250,000 people heard Martin Luther King Jr. deliver his famous "I Have a Dream" speech.

Nonviolent protesters were sometimes met with brutal violence, but the protesters' actions led to important changes. The Civil Rights Act of 1964 ended segregation and made it illegal for businesses to discriminate against people based on their race, sex, or religion. The Voting Rights Act of 1965 made it harder for Southern states to deny black citizens the right to vote.

In New York, Aretha continued recording albums with John Hammond for Columbia. She recorded new versions of other people's songs, but she also sang some original tunes.

Aretha never forgot her gospel roots. "Nobody Like You" appeared on her second Columbia album, *The Electrifying Aretha Franklin*. The song was written by James Cleveland, the leader of C.L.'s choir at New Bethel Baptist Church. One of the musicians who worked on the song told Aretha he couldn't believe it had been written by a church man. "Joe," Aretha told him, "it's all church." Like her father, Aretha believed that all good music came from God.

In late 1963, Dinah Washington, "Queen of the Blues," died at the young age of thirty-nine. Aretha had always looked up to Dinah, a talented performer who had been close with Reverend Franklin.

Dinah Washington

Ted thought Aretha could be "the new Dinah." He wanted Aretha to record a tribute album to Dinah, and Aretha agreed. So only one month after Aretha and Ted had their first child together, Ted Jr., they were back at work in the studio.

Unforgettable: A Tribute to Dinah Washington, is one of Aretha's classic albums, and one of the best she ever recorded for Columbia. It is filled with emotion—sad, sweet, and powerful. Unfortunately, the album did not produce a hit single. Aretha's contract with Columbia was almost up, and she felt that time was running out for her to have a hit song on the charts.

Ted and Aretha were not getting along. Ted became very controlling. The two separated for a while. Aretha spent the summer of 1965 in Detroit with her family. Even after returning to New York, she traveled to Detroit to see her sons every few weeks.

For Aretha, five years with Columbia Records had produced eight albums but no hits. Although she had been working very hard, her father's

advice about recording with Columbia hadn't seemed to work out the way they had hoped. Sad and lonely in New York City, she dreamed about a day when things would be better. But would that day ever come?

CHAPTER 5
"I Want Hits"

The 1960s were a time of changing tastes in music. In the 1950s, the great jazz musicians were already well established. By presenting her to the country as a jazz and blues singer, Columbia had made Aretha seem old-fashioned. Music fans in the sixties wanted to rock and roll. They wanted to dance.

Unforgettable was released the same year the Beatles had taken America by storm. Motown acts like the Temptations had crossed over with big pop hits like "My Girl." It was an exciting time for pop music, but Columbia was marketing Aretha—with her mature, grown-up voice—to an older, mostly black, audience.

Atlantic Records was a smaller, friendlier company than Columbia. Atlantic was owned by two brothers from Turkey and two New Yorkers.

Jerry Wexler, Nesuhi Ertegun, and Ahmet Ertegun

The men not only owned the record label, they also produced their artists' music. They ran most parts of the business themselves, from recording to promoting their artists around the country.

Atlantic specialized in a new kind of music called "soul," which combined elements of R&B, pop, and rock—and added a good dose of *feeling*! It was music that expressed a lot of emotion. And if Aretha could do one thing really well, it was sing with emotion and *soul*!

When Jerry Wexler—one of the owners of Atlantic—heard that Aretha Franklin was unhappy at Columbia, he wanted her to know that Atlantic would be happy to have her.

In 1966, they set up a meeting in Jerry Wexler's Manhattan office. At the meeting, Jerry asked Aretha what kind of music she wanted to record.

"I want hits," she told him.

They made a deal right then and there.

Aretha and Ted were working together again. They wanted to record in New York, like they always had. But Jerry Wexler wanted to record at FAME Studios in Muscle Shoals, a small town

in northern Alabama near the Tennessee border. Unlike the well-rehearsed Columbia recording sessions, at FAME, the music wouldn't be prepared ahead of time. The musicians there—a group of white country artists—had a looser, morc flcxiblc stylc.

In the 1960s, the United States was a very racially divided nation, particularly in the South. Aretha wasn't so sure about traveling to record there. But Jerry Wexler called Muscle Shoals a "soul paradise." And so Aretha and Ted agreed to record in Alabama.

In January 1967, the Muscle Shoals recording sessions began. Aretha came prepared. She had an original song, "Dr. Feelgood," plus one she'd written with her sister Carolyn, called "Baby Baby Baby." The first song she wanted to record, "I Never Loved a Man (The Way I Love You)," had been written by one of Ted's clients.

The Muscle Shoals Sound

The traditional blues of black people and white country music came together in Muscle Shoals, Alabama, to create a new, hip, and soulful sound. The "Muscle Shoals sound" featured heavy drums and bass guitar. And people loved it. This sound was best captured by a group called the Swampers, the band who worked at FAME Studios.

Rick Hall cofounded FAME in 1959 and formed the Swampers by hiring local musicians. They weren't formally trained, but they had a unique sound, great instincts, and a lot of soul. The Swampers eventually left FAME to open another studio across town. Artists like Little Richard, the Rolling Stones, Bob Dylan, Lynyrd Skynyrd, and Carrie Underwood have all recorded in Muscle Shoals.

The first day in the studio, Aretha was shy. She called all the musicians "Mister," so they called her "Miss Franklin." It was all very formal. And Aretha was quiet. Nobody quite knew how to start the song.

Then one of the musicians played some opening chords on the electric piano and blew everyone away—including Aretha.

Aretha sat at the other piano and began to sing, and the band came to life. Aretha felt their energy. Everyone became giddy and excited.

They could tell Aretha was going to be a star! About twenty minutes later, they had recorded the song.

Everyone knew they had a smash hit with

"I Never Loved a Man." The song is about a man who is a liar and a cheater. The woman singing the song doesn't understand why she still loves him.

Two of the musicians quickly wrote a new song right there in the studio. They began recording "Do Right Woman, Do Right Man" that same day. The song sounds like a response to "I Never Loved a Man." The lyrics say that a man has to be a good person in order to be loved in return by a good woman.

At the end of the day, everyone was in a great mood. Unfortunately, Ted got into an argument with one of the horn players and the studio owner. It was a terrible end to a wonderful day.

Ted was angry with Jerry Wexler. He told him Muscle Shoals was far from a "soul paradise" and that Aretha might never record for Atlantic again. He and Aretha left Alabama. Jerry was upset. He worried that their great recording would never be heard!

Aretha went home to Detroit. Ted flew back to New York. Aretha was angry with Ted, and she wouldn't return Jerry Wexler's calls.

Jerry *knew* that "I Never Loved a Man" would be a huge hit. But he couldn't release a record without another song. He needed a "B" side. Singles were seven-inch vinyl records that had an "A side"—the hit song—and a second song on the "B side." That day in Muscle Shoals, they had recorded only part of "Do Right Woman, Do Right Man." It wasn't finished yet.

With Aretha ignoring his calls, Jerry Wexler decided to do something a little bit risky. Without telling anyone, he made a couple dozen copies of "I Never Loved a Man" and sent them out to DJs around the country. Listeners went crazy for the song! They called their radio stations, asking where they could buy the record. But there was no record to buy!

Finally, after ten days, Aretha called Jerry back.

"Mr. Wexler," she said, "I'm ready to record."

She told him she wouldn't return to Muscle Shoals. She wanted to record in New York. But she wanted the Southern musicians. "They understood me," she said. Aretha asked Jerry to bring them up to the city.

Just two days after "Do Right Woman" was recorded, Aretha's first single for Atlantic, "I Never Loved a Man," was released with "Do Right Woman" on the B side. Within two weeks, it had sold 250,000 copies, and would go on to be Aretha's first-ever million-selling record. It immediately shot up to number one on the R&B charts.

But most exciting for Aretha, "I Never Loved a Man" rose to the top ten on the pop charts. She finally had her crossover hit! This was the moment Aretha had been waiting for.

She was no longer a jazz or blues artist singing for a black audience. Now everyone in America, black *and* white, knew Aretha's name—and they couldn't wait for more of her songs.

CHAPTER 6
R-E-S-P-E-C-T!

In the Atlantic recording studios in New York, Aretha and the Muscle Shoals band continued their work. Aretha had a new song she had been performing live called "Respect." It was by a musician named Otis Redding.

Otis Redding

When Otis Redding heard Aretha's rendition of his song, he smiled and said, "The girl has taken that song from me. Ain't no longer my song." Then he asked to hear it again.

Aretha sings "Respect" so forcefully, she

practically shouts. She sings with such power and authority that it doesn't sound like she's *asking* for respect . . . she's *demanding* it!

"Respect" hit the charts on April 29, 1967. It became an instant hit.

Many people in late-1960s America were demanding respect for themselves and fighting for civil rights, women's rights, and gay rights. America was in the middle of a long and bloody war in Vietnam, and many young people no longer trusted their government. Revolution was in the air.

"Respect" became the anthem of a generation, and Aretha's biggest hit. In less than two months, it had reached number one on both the R&B *and* pop charts, and the top ten in England!

During a concert at Chicago's Regal Theater a few months later, Aretha was named the Queen of Soul by a local DJ. A crown with jewels was placed on her head. Aretha was now a member of music "royalty" alongside Mahalia Jackson,

Dinah Washington, and Sam Cooke. Aretha took the honor seriously.

At another concert, in 1968, the mayor of Detroit declared February 16 "Aretha Franklin Day." Martin Luther King Jr. attended the ceremony. It was the last time Aretha would see Dr. King.

Now that the Queen had hit the big-time, she worked even harder. She toured constantly. She released two albums every year, but she recorded enough music for even more than that!

Aretha's third and fourth albums for Atlantic, *Lady Soul* and *Aretha Now*, were released in 1968. The albums produced three major hits for Aretha: "Chain of Fools," "(You Make Me Feel Like) A Natural Woman," and "Think."

Aretha and Ted were still married, but their relationship was difficult. In "Chain of Fools," Aretha could have been singing about her own life. She tells the story of a cruel man who has treated her badly.

"Natural Woman" is a romantic ballad about a sad woman whose life changes completely when the right man comes along. Aretha said the "man" in that song was God.

“Think” is a fast and furious song. In the chorus, Aretha sings “Freedom!” eight times, the notes going higher and louder each time. Her cries for freedom gave her fans the same soulful joy that “Respect” had.

Aretha’s star had risen. Requests for TV and concert appearances poured in. The Queen of Soul was in high demand.

In May of 1968, Aretha left for her first concert tour of Europe. Her concert in Paris was recorded

for a live album. In Amsterdam, she opened her show with a cover of the Rolling Stones' rock 'n' roll hit "(I Can't Get No) Satisfaction." Fans threw flowers onstage to welcome her. She ended the night with a super-fast version of "Respect." In Stockholm, the crown prince and princess of Sweden came to her show. Aretha surprised the crowd with an old Broadway tune, "There's No Business Like Show Business."

Aretha's live shows were exciting, and the crowds were wild. With her large, talented band and energetic backup singers, Aretha offered her fans something they couldn't get on her records: an up-close-and-personal experience with the raw emotions of her soulful style.

Back home in the States, Aretha appeared on the cover of *TIME* magazine. She performed to more than twenty thousand fans at New York's Madison Square Garden. Aretha and Ted had split up for good. Aretha's brother, Cecil, became her new manager.

In early 1969, Aretha met someone new. Ken E. Cunningham was kind and handsome, and Aretha was in love. In March 1970, she gave birth to her fourth son, Kecalf. Ken and Aretha came up with his name (pronounced "Kalph") by combining their initials, "K.E.C." and "A.L.F."

Aretha was successful, happy, and healthy. Those "better days" she had dreamed about after leaving her old record label had finally arrived.

CHAPTER 7
Amazing Grace

About a month after Kecalf was born, Aretha returned to the studio. She had written some new songs while she was pregnant. Her standout, gospel-inspired song "Spirit in the Dark," became the name of the new album.

Jerry Wexler described the song as "Aretha conducting church right in the middle of [a] smoky nightclub."

In 1972, Aretha decided to hold a church service of her own—and record it for a live album. She hadn't recorded a gospel album since she was a teenager. Aretha was almost thirty now, and it was time for her to go back to her roots.

The album *Amazing Grace* was recorded over two nights in January at the New Temple Missionary Baptist Church in Los Angeles. The service was conducted by Reverend James Cleveland, C.L.'s old choir director from Detroit. Jerry Wexler brought in his band of musicians.

Reverend Cleveland reminded the audience that this was to be a true religious service. Still, he invited them to "get into the spirit" and to make their voices heard for the recording.

Aretha performed a mix of religious and popular songs. But the pop songs had a religious message. She sang Marvin Gaye's "Wholy Holy" and Clara Ward's "How I Got Over." Toward the end of "What a Friend We Have in Jesus," Aretha mixed in a bit of the pop song "You've Got a Friend."

Aretha's childhood idol Clara Ward was in the front row, sitting next to Aretha's father. While Aretha played at the piano during "God Will Take Care of You," Reverend Franklin came to the stage to wipe the sweat from his daughter's forehead. It was a sweet and tender moment.

Some people didn't agree with Aretha's decision

to record pop songs in a church. When they heard that Mick Jagger, the lead singer for the Rolling Stones, was in the audience, they said Aretha was just putting on this show for the attention. But Reverend Cleveland, like Aretha and her father, believed that "it's all God's music, and it's all good." And Carolyn Franklin said, "I'm telling you that it was real. It was righteous." She meant that Aretha's intentions were honorable and pure.

The event was "righteous" indeed. Aretha had come back to the church to thank the Lord for her musical gift. She gave a stirring and powerful performance.

Amazing Grace was released at a trying time for black America. Martin Luther King Jr., Malcolm X, and Bobby Kennedy, all champions for civil rights, had been assassinated. The Vietnam War raged on. Cecil said that, with *Amazing Grace*, "Aretha helped lead us back to God." The album went on to sell more than two million copies, Aretha's best-selling album ever!

CHAPTER 8
Jump to It

Aretha continued recording albums with Atlantic. Her next hit album, *Sparkle*, came out in 1976. America's taste in music was changing again. Disco, with its steady and danceable beats, was all the rage. Aretha's next big hits wouldn't come until the 1980s.

In 1975, Aretha moved to Southern California with Ken and her four sons. But Aretha and Ken broke up soon after the move. Aretha's sister Carolyn moved in with her and the boys for a while. Aretha was hoping to get into the movies. Then she met someone new.

Glynn Turman was a handsome actor with three children of his own. He had starred in a TV soap opera called *Peyton Place*. Aretha and Glynn were married by Reverend Franklin at New Bethel Baptist Church in 1978. Their wedding was very fancy. Their wedding cake stood eight feet tall!

In June 1979, tragedy struck the Franklin family. C.L. was shot during a robbery in his own home. Aretha's father lay unconscious in a coma for the next several years. He needed around-the-clock home care. Aretha paid his medical bills, of course, but she would have to work as hard as ever.

In 1980, Aretha appeared in the movie *The Blues Brothers.* Aretha played Mrs. Murphy, a waitress who runs a diner with her husband. Her husband wants to leave the diner to go on tour with his old band. Aretha sang "Think" to him—

"Think about what you're trying to do to me!"—and audiences loved it!

Clive Davis

In 1979, Aretha was awarded a star on the Hollywood Walk of Fame, and in 1980, she signed with a new record label, Arista Records. Clive Davis was the president of the company. He was known as a hit maker. Aretha wanted another hit record, and Clive was the man to help her record it.

Clive introduced Aretha to Luther Vandross, one of the hottest singer-songwriters at the time. Luther was proud of the musicians he worked with. He described their style as "silky-smooth with just a taste of the dance-disco-dazzle." When Aretha came in to record, Luther said "she completely burned it up and set the studio on fire." Luther was cool, but Aretha had *soul*!

The first single and title song on the 1982 album *Jump to It* became Aretha's first number one hit in five years. *Get It Right* followed in 1983. The title song from that album also went to number one. In 1985, "Freeway of Love" became Aretha's biggest hit since "Respect" and her first song to hit number one on the dance charts. In 1987, she became the first woman inducted into the Rock and Roll Hall of Fame.

Aretha, now in her forties, was back on top.

CHAPTER 9
The Queen of Soul

Aretha moved back to Detroit in 1982. Despite her recent recording successes, times were tough. She had developed a fear of flying and rarely left the city. She and Glynn divorced in 1984.

The next five years were filled with sadness. Aretha's father passed away, and then she lost her sister Carolyn to breast cancer in 1988. Shortly after Carolyn died, her grandmother, Big Mama, and her brother, Cecil, died as well. These were difficult years for Aretha.

Her family meant everything to her, especially her beloved father. He had recognized Aretha's gift from an early age and helped put her on the path to success.

But the Queen would go on. There didn't seem to be a song she couldn't sing.

Aretha began performing opera songs during some of her live shows. At the 40th annual Grammy Awards in 1998, the famous opera singer Luciano Pavarotti became ill and could not perform. Aretha stepped in at the last minute, singing a song called "Nessun Dorma" in Italian. As she belted out the closing notes, the audience leaped to their feet and gave her a standing ovation.

Later that year, Aretha appeared alongside Gloria Estefan, Shania Twain, Mariah Carey, and Celine Dion at the Beacon Theatre in New York City for VH1's *Divas Live*, a TV concert special. Proceeds from the concert went to Save the Music

Foundation, which donates money to help school music programs.

What Is a Diva?

Opera singer Maria Callas

Diva comes from the Latin word for "goddess." In Italian, it can refer to a female opera singer. Another opera term for *diva* is *prima donna*, which means "first lady." These singers are the very best at what they do: singing long, difficult parts in dramatic operas.

In popular culture today, the word *diva* usually means a talented female entertainer, and sometimes refers to an actual legendary personality.

Divas can have reputations for being highly demanding, difficult to work with, and competitive. They want to be the best, and they want their fans to know it!

At *Divas Live*, Aretha sang "Chain of Fools" with Mariah Carey. For the show's finale, all five women sang "Natural Woman" along with Carole King, who had cowritten the song for Aretha in the 1960s. As the song drew to a close, Aretha danced her way across the stage in front of the others. She threw her hands to the sky as she cried out the closing notes. Those notes were *hers* to sing!

In 2005, Aretha was awarded the Presidential Medal of Freedom by George W. Bush to honor her contribution to American music and culture. And in 2009, Aretha was proud to sing "My Country 'Tis of Thee" at the inauguration of Barack Obama, America's first black president.

Aretha wore a gray felt hat with a huge bow, which she'd had specially lined with sparkly rhinestones. People talked about her attention-grabbing hat on the Internet for days!

In 2010, *Rolling Stone* magazine named Aretha the greatest singer of all time, calling her "a gift from God." Four years later, the Queen of Soul released an album featuring her own versions of popular modern songs like Adele's "Rolling in the Deep," and classics like Gloria Gaynor's "I Will Survive."

For more than sixty years, Aretha's music spanned all styles—from gospel and jazz to soul and pop. She erased the lines between black and white music and made fans across all generations. Aretha continued to record music and perform concerts around the United States until announcing her retirement in 2017. She passed away in 2018 at the age of seventy-six.

Aretha Franklin was already a legend as a teenage gospel singer. She became one of the most revered and *respected* voices in American music. And she alone sits atop her throne, as the one and only Queen of Soul.

Timeline of Aretha Franklin's Life

1942	Aretha Louise Franklin is born in Memphis, Tennessee
1946	Moves to Detroit, Michigan
1948	Aretha's mother and half brother move to Buffalo
1952	Mother dies of heart attack
	Sings first solo in church
1956	Releases first album, *Songs of Faith*
1960	Moves to New York, signs with Columbia Records
1961	Marries first husband, Ted White
1966	Signs with Atlantic Records
1967	Records "I Never Loved a Man" in Muscle Shoals
	"Respect" hits number one on the pop and R&B charts
	Crowned the Queen of Soul
1972	*Amazing Grace*, Aretha's best-selling album, is released
1975	Moves to California with Ken E. Cunningham and her sons
1978	Marries second husband, Glynn Turman
1980	Appears in a movie, *The Blues Brothers*
	Signs with Arista Records
1987	Inducted into the Rock and Roll Hall of Fame
2005	Awarded the Presidential Medal of Freedom
2009	Performs at the presidential inauguration of Barack Obama
2010	Named greatest singer of all time by *Rolling Stone*
2017	Aretha announces she will retire at age seventy-five
2018	Dies in Detroit on August 16

Timeline of the World

1942	Movie *Casablanca* premieres in New York City
1946	New type of bathing suit, the bikini, goes on sale in Paris
1948	First Polaroid camera goes on sale in Boston
1954	US Supreme Court, in its *Brown v. Board of Education* decision, declares state laws segregating public schools unconstitutional
1955	Rosa Parks refuses to give up her seat on the bus to a white man in Montgomery, Alabama
1962	The Beatles record their first single, "Love Me Do"
1966	The Beach Boys top the charts with their song "Good Vibrations"
1967	Green Bay Packers and Kansas City Chiefs play Super Bowl I
1968	Martin Luther King Jr. is assassinated in Memphis, Tennessee
1971	Walt Disney World opens outside Orlando, Florida
1975	Vietnam War ends
1981	MTV airs its first music video, "Video Killed the Radio Star" by the Buggles
	Beyoncé Knowles is born in Houston, Texas
1985	Nintendo Entertainment System goes on sale in the US
2005	YouTube is founded
2009	Michael Jackson, the King of Pop, dies
2017	Donald J. Trump becomes the forty-fifth president of the US

Bibliography

*** Books for young readers**

Franklin, Aretha, and David Ritz. ***Aretha: From These Roots.*** New York: Villard, 1999.

*Gourse, Leslie. ***Aretha Franklin: Lady Soul***. New York: Franklin Watts, 1995.

Muscle Shoals. Directed by Greg "Freddy" Camalier. Magnolia Pictures, 2013.

Ritz, David. ***Respect: The Life of Aretha Franklin.*** New York: Little, Brown and Company, 2014.

Werner, Craig. ***A Change Is Gonna Come: Music, Race & the Soul of America.*** New York: Plume, 1998.